POMPOUS T. DADCHILD

101 REASONS WHY

USD is better than Bitcoin

Summary

Premise

Bitcoin was the most relevant scam in the history of money, even more absurd of that gold thing.

Luckily, now Bitcoin is dead. It died may times, almost 330 according to 99bitcoins.com, I have to be honest, but now is really dead.

I could say: "It's dead because everyone tells it is", but the members of that crazy Bitcoin cult (bitcoiners, bitcoin maximalist and shitcoin minimalist) would say: " I don't care what people says". Anarchists.

So I will argue my statement and I will also prove that US dollar is a better form of money, even if an individual of sound principles and average intelligence would not need my explaination.

Let's proceed with order with a little bit of history.

As you probably know, exchanges of value between individuals began with barter. I create a product A, you make a product B; if I need B and you need A we can exchange our products.

But there is a problem, and is called double coincidence of wants.

Double coincidence of wants means that both parties have to agree to sell and buy each products. The problem is caused by the improbability of the wants, needs, or events that cause or motivate a transaction occurring at the same time and the same place.

So we found something else: commodity money.

Commodity money consists of objects that have intrinsic value, durability, and, often, scarcity.

But there was a problem. People began holding these commodities, especially gold, instead of spend them and make debts with the central authority!

We had to find something else.

Why didn't we represent these commodity with paper? Oh, we did!

And even better. In 1971, after an incredible research on how to limit the purchasing power of the individual and concentrate it in the hands of the State, finally United States' President Richard Nixon, with his Nixon Shock measures, decided for an unilateral cancellation of the direct international convertibility of the United States Dollar to gold.

The State won.

Or not?

In 2008 a unknow scammer, named Satoshi Nakamoto, probably under the influence of drugs, gave birth to what seemed initially only an idea that was going to solve a problem that did not exist, but then turned out to be the biggest economic fraud in the history of mankind.

Our lovely State and Order were in danger.

And so, this is why it was necessary to write this book: to prove, once and for all, that USD (and FIAT in general) is better than Bitcoin.

Reason 1

Reason 2

Reason 3

Reason 4

Reason 5

Reason 6

Reason 7

Reason 8

Reason 9

Reason 10

Reason 11

Reason 12

Reason 13

Reason 14

Reason 15

Reason 16

Reason 17

Reason 18

Reason 19

Reason 20

Reason 21

Reason 22

Reason 23

Reason 24

Reason 28

Reason 26

Reason 27

Reason 28

Reason 29

Reason 30

Reason 31

Reason 32

Reason 33

Reason 34

Reason 35

Reason 36

Reason 37

Reason 38

Reason 39

Reason 40

Reason 41

Reason 42

Reason 43

Reason 44

Reason 45

Reason 46

Reason 47

Reason 48

Reason 49

Reason 50

Reason 51

Reason 52

Reason 53

Reason 54

Reason 55

Reason 56

Reason 57

Reason 58

Reason 59

Reason 60

Reason 61

Reason 62

Reason 63

Reason 64

Reason 65

Reason 66

Reason 67

Reason 68

Reason 69

Reason 70

Reason 71

Reason 72

Reason 73

Reason 74

Reason 75

Reason 76

Reason 77

Reason 78

Reason 79

Reason 80

Reason 81

Reason 82

Reason 83

Reason 84

Reason 85

Reason 86

Reason 87

Reason 88

Reason 89

Reason 90

Reason 91

Reason 92

Reason 93

Reason 94

Reason 95

Reason 96

Reason 97

Reason 98

Reason 99

Reason 100

Reason 101

Conclusion

And this is why USD is better than Bitcoin.

If you think these are unequivocal reasons and you want to save your State, please take some useless bitcoin (BTC) and send it to this address:
bc1qlvgsv52de3e7mlhs4l9c2635hrjgutaeg4dl2a

You will do your part for a better old World.